Stop Loving Them So Much

A Practical Guide to Raising an Adult You Actually Like

By
Jennifer Sterling

Stop Loving Them So Much

ISBN: 979-8-9946927-1-4

Disclaimer: This book is intended for educational and personal tracking purposes only. The author and publisher are not engaged in rendering legal, accounting, or financial investment advice.

Published by Sterling Bridge Media

Contents

Introduction: The Hard Truth

If you've picked up this book, I already know a few things about you. You're exhausted. You're frustrated. And deep down, you're feeling a specific kind of guilt that you don't talk about.

You love your kids. You've tried to give them everything. You've been their cheerleader, their chauffeur, their ATM, and their safety net. But now they're hovering on the edge of adulthood—or maybe they've already crossed over—and something is wrong. The "return on investment" isn't what you expected. Instead of a confident, capable adult, you're looking at someone who still expects you to do the heavy lifting.

I'm here to tell you that the problem is not just them. It's the "Loving Too Much" trap.

Sometime around the mid-60s parents were told that being a "good parent" meant removing every obstacle. Parents thought they were protecting their children, but they were actually keeping them from developing the very muscles needed to survive in the real world. Kids sought escapes from responsibility—alcohol, sex, drugs or gangs. They traded long-term goals and the discipline of "doing without" for the hollow promise of instant gratification. By the 80s and 90s, kids were aging out of childhood and into adulthood totally lacking the tools for self-sufficiency. They lived with mom and dad and ran up debt they couldn't repay. No call/No show became an everyday occurrence in the workforce as they indulged their desires and neglected their responsibilities.

Parents had been so busy being "supportive" that they'd forgotten to be the trainer.

This book isn't a lecture on "tough love"—I *hate* that phrase. This is a manual on **Tactical Parenting**. It's about shifting your role from the person who fixes everything to the person who prepares them for anything!

In the pages that follow, we're going to look at the parenting **Pillars**: Motivation, Boundary, Penalty, and Action. These aren't just corporate buzzwords; they are the framework for a relationship that actually works. We're going to talk about how to stop reacting to their "emergencies" and start responding with a plan that can help them learn to solve their own problems.

I'm not promising that this will be easy. In fact, some of it is going to feel counterintuitive. It's going to feel "mean" to say no when you have the power to say yes. But remember: your job isn't to make them happy today. Your job is to make them capable forever.

It took me a long time to realize that by doing everything for them, I was actually telling them I didn't think they could do it for themselves. It's time to change that narrative. It's time to stop loving them "so much" that you're holding them back.

Let's get to work.

Chapter 1: The Love Trap

(Stop Loving Them So Much)

How many times a day do we use the word "love"? We love our jobs, our dogs, our cars, and our homes. We love chocolate, movies, pink roses, and long walks. In short, we use the word "love" for anything that makes us feel good.

The modern definition of love has become convoluted, and that confusion is dangerous when it comes to raising children. If your definition of love is tied to "warm fuzzies" and avoiding discomfort, you are going to struggle with the most important part of the job: discipline.

Love as a Responsibility

True love isn't a feeling; it is doing what is best and right for someone else. More often than not, doing what is right is difficult and painful. It requires a level of "negativeness" that makes most parents uncomfortable.

The hard truth is that the basic factor for failing to be a good parent is **selfishness**. It shows up in two ways:

1. Being unwilling to give up your own time and desires to deal with your children.
2. Refusing to discipline because the conflict is too painful for *you* to handle.

We have to move past our own needs and realize that if WE don't take control and lead, our children definitely will. How many times have you been in a grocery store behind a child in the cart ahead of you who is screaming – not crying, SCREAMING? Mom knows you're watching and can feel your disapproval. So, what does she do? She picks up the candy the child wants and gives it to him.

The Message? If you scream and embarrass me loud enough and long enough, you get what you want.

A better response would be to pull your cart out of line and remove the child from the store. I know, it's an added layer of "pain" to your day, but the real truth is we just don't want to deal with the headache of a tantrum. That's not love; that's taking the easy way out … at the child's expense!

NOTE: There's a difference between an unruly or "spoiled" child and one that has a condition, e.g., autism, that can manifest itself in these types of behaviors. As an onlooker, we may not know the actual reason for the outburst. Error on the side of "cutting the parent some slack". As the parent, however, it is our responsibility to seek professional guidance that will help us *and* the child.

Training vs. Punishment

When I talk about discipline, I'm not talking about just dropping the hammer or physical punishment. I'm talking about **Training, Instructing and Educating**.

- **Training** them to make good choices.
- **Instructing** them in acceptable manners and behaviors.
- **Educating** them against the dangers and evils that live in our world.

Does that sound easy? If it were easy, more parents would be doing it. It requires time, energy, and constant repetition. It means doing all the things we *must* do—working, shopping, cleaning—and then finding the strength to cut back on the things we *want* to do so we can be present for our children.

The "Two-Strike" Rule

You have to ask yourself: Who is running the show? Is it the parent, or the child?

Here is my first rule: **If a parent has to say it more than twice, the child is in control**.

Parenting is an often-painful experience, but it is the only way to reach the reward of raising a respectable citizen. Don't get me wrong, there are no guarantees. These miniature humans have a mind of their own. But our influence plays a huge part in developing their personalities and beliefs. And it starts with showing up. It doesn't matter if it's the television from my generation or the cell phone in yours—if your eyes are on a screen, they aren't on your child. You have to decide if your child's future is more important than your current comfort.

Chapter 2: The Three Pillars of Training

If you've accepted that love is doing what is right rather than what feels good, you are ready for the "nuts and bolts" of raising a respectable citizen. In my two decades of on-the-job training, I've found that effective parenting rests on three pillars: **Training, Instruction, and Education.**

Too many people hear the word "discipline" and think only of punishment—dropping the hammer after a rule is broken. But real discipline is multifaceted. It's about instinct, preparedness, and order. We discipline our bodies through exercise and our pets through repetition; we must discipline our children as well.

Pillar 1: Training for Choice

We are responsible for "training up" our children. This means giving them the tools to make a good choice before they are faced with a bad one.

The Two-Strike Rule: I mentioned this concept in Chapter One. It's the most basic level of training, and it starts with your voice. If you have to say something more than twice, the child is in control. You have to ask yourself: "Who is running the show? The parent or the child?". If you allow yourself to be ignored, you aren't training them to listen; you're training them that your words don't have weight. At two-years old it's a question of danger and boundaries. As a teenager, the stakes are raised dramatically—they can be life changing.

The second time you speak, you're not just repeating yourself; you're giving a warning. If you have to speak a third time, the 'training' moves to 'consequences.' You don't yell, and you don't negotiate. You simply go to the **Discipline Inventory** (which we will build at the end of this chapter) and utilize a consequence from the 'Hate List.' When the child knows the third strike is automatic, they start listening at strike one.

Pillar 2: Instruction in Behaviors

Instruction is about setting the standard for how to move through the world. This is where we teach acceptable manners and social behaviors.

The Mirror Method (Experiential Discipline): Sometimes, verbal instruction isn't enough, and the "punishment must fit the crime". For example, at around 12 or 13 years old, my son was constantly flipping people off. It was nasty and disrespectful. But I didn't yell at him. I wanted the punishment to fit the crime. So, I set up a full-sized mirror and made him watch himself repeatedly flip *himself* off. I made it clear that this was not about humiliating him. **It was about letting him see what the rest of us were seeing.** It was about self-awareness. When he was caught spitting at people, he had to spit on his own reflection in that same mirror. He was experiencing the behavior first hand. And believe me, he hated that!! **Instruction works best when the child experiences the reality of their behavior.**

So, did the discipline work? Well, he didn't and doesn't spit at people since that time. As for "the finger"? Don't really know. I never caught him and no one complained about it. But honestly, it's such a common gesture these days, I wouldn't be surprised if he did.

Here's the thing, I can only do what I can do. I can't follow him around every day to ensure his behaviors are acceptable (to me). I can only teach, provide positive/negative reinforcements, and pray!

Pillar 3: Education Against the World

Finally, we must educate our children against the dangers and evils of the world. Many parents try to shield their children from the world, but in doing so, we fail to teach them.

The message must be: "I am your parent, and I love you more than my own life. But…

If *I* will not put up with this behavior, society certainly won't".

We try to educate them so they can learn the hard lessons at the lower end of the spectrum, saving them from the major troubles they cannot outlive or overcome later. Whether it's the actual breaking of a law or perhaps the threat of "calling CPS/police because they don't like the rules, you address the "bluff" directly. Something like: If your child threatens to call the law because you've taken their phone, your answer should be: 'Here, use my phone. If you think the state will provide you a better life than I do, feel free.' When they realize you aren't afraid of their 'weapons,' those weapons lose their power.

The Discipline Inventory

To make this work, you have to know what matters to your child. I recommend having your child make a list of the following:

- **Four or five things they love (positive reinforcement):** (e.g., Slumber parties, movies, new clothes).
- **Four or five things they hate (negative consequences):** (e.g., Writing sentences, early bedtime, no TV).

Use this list. If they follow the training, they are rewarded with the things they love. If they break the rules, the consequence comes from the list of things they hate. It takes the guess-work out of parenting and puts the power of the outcome squarely in the child's hands.

But don't be fooled. The positive reinforcements will be genuine—they want these! But the negative consequences may have to have a few iterations to get to the final list. If they don't list appropriate negative consequences, just tell them you can fill in that portion of the list!!

By the way, these lists are "living documents". When the child outgrows items on the list, like slumber parties, they will need an updated positive reinforcement list. The same is true of the negative consequences list.

Chapter 3: The Cost of Commitment

(Time, Energy, and the Single Parent's Marathon)

If the previous chapters felt heavy, it's because the truth is heavy. Real parenting is not a hobby; it is a precious commodity of time and energy. It requires doing all the things we *must* do—working long hours, shopping, cleaning, yard work, car maintenance—and then finding the energy for everything else.

The Energy Audit

Sometimes I thought I had used my allotted supply of energy for a lifetime. I worked all day, rushed home to cook and clean, and prepared to do it all over again the next day. There were days when I felt I didn't have energy for anything more.

But here is where the commitment was tested: we have to demonstrate commitment to our children, not just pay lip-service to it. This means:

- **Reviewing homework and checking chores** even when you're exhausted.
- **Turning off the television and putting down the phone** and reclaiming that time.
- **Listening more than talking** during one-on-one time with your child.

I don't know about you, but I'm dog-tired just remembering those days. But I got through it, and you will too!

The Weight of the World Alone

As a single parent, I felt the weight of the world on *my* shoulders alone. I had a full-time job, a part-time job, and every single household and maintenance task. If you are in this position, you have to stay on top of discipline even more fiercely.

When my children were about 11 and 12 years old, my job dictated that I start work at 6:00 AM. I had to rely on my kids to get themselves to school on their own and act appropriately. My rule was hard and fast:

If you get in trouble with a teacher or a babysitter, you get double trouble at home.

This wasn't meant as a power play. As a single parent, I had to rely on my children to be responsible and follow the rules. I couldn't sit in the classroom with them. The '*Double Trouble'* rule was my **proxy**. It was always there to remind them there are consequences (positive and negative) for their actions. You have to maintain control even when you aren't physically in the room.

Let me demonstrate what I mean. My daughter, we'll call her Susan, was always a handful. She wanted to see everything and do everything. It took massive effort to just keep her grounded. In the seventh grade, the issues became even more intense. I found myself sitting in the principal's office at her middle school listening to a teacher say, "Susan is the most disrespectful child I have ever dealt with." I was humiliated and, frankly, really ticked off! With all the time and effort I was putting in on raising my children, this was the end result?

After about an hour I finally asked the teacher what he felt a satisfactory punishment would be. He said two weeks of detention and a one-page paper on being respectful. That sounded good to me. I turned to my daughter who was sitting uncharacteristically silent in a corner—*was it because she knew the 'Double Trouble' rule was about to hit her like a ton of bricks?* I asked her to explain the rule about trouble at school. She did. Basically, she would have two weeks of detention and a paper to write at school, and four weeks of "detention" and another paper to write at home.

Does that sound excessive? It did to me, but that was the whole idea. Susan needed to get the message loud and clear the first time, because I didn't want to go through it again. Besides, her younger brother was in the background watching and listening. I wanted him to get the message too.

Fast forward a week. Susan is doing her detention and finished her one-page paper for school. That Friday the teacher sent home a note that said, "I think Susan has paid her debt to society. I feel like she can be released from detention early." I sent a note back to school on Monday saying his decision was fine with me, but she would complete the entire four weeks at home. I didn't want to do this again!

We had a family meeting that weekend and discussed both the teacher's decision and mine. I felt it was important for both kids to understand my decision to complete the entire course. It wasn't about being angry or embarrassed. It was about building character and taking responsibility.

Of course, Susan was not happy with my decision to complete the entire four weeks of home detention, but she did complete it! Funny thing was, at her school's open house several weeks later, I found out that same teacher had become her favorite teacher and vise versa. She helped him clean up the classroom after school and once she even did a "voluntary" detention because he was the one on duty. Kids are strange!

Eating the Encyclopedia

I don't want you to think you will be successful every time. Believe me, you will fail. You will lose your cool, you will set a rule you can't enforce, and you will eventually have to swallow your pride. Let go of the guilt and the expectation of perfection. Go ahead and eat that encyclopedia.

One of *my* biggest regrets is putting so much pressure on my kids to get it right that I forgot to acknowledge that they *tried* to get it right. I needed to cut them some slack…but I needed to cut myself some as well.

I munched on my encyclopedia of "my kids won't" just like you will. Believe me, your kids *will*. Don't be embarrassed; we all eat that book in some form. The goal isn't to be a perfect parent; it's to be a present one. And being present means having the guts to stay in the marathon when every muscle in your body wants to quit. You aren't just raising a child; you're building a citizen. And that kind of work is never done in your "spare time."

Chapter 4: Finding Time for Quality Time

(Communication is Key)

Perhaps the best way to discuss quality time is to tell you what I'm *not* talking about. I'm not talking about going to the movies, spending time at the mall, or sitting in front of the television. You may be present, but you're not communicating. And you are not *listening* to the child. The reason these activities don't qualify is that they require no one-on-one communication and no eye contact between you and your child.

It's not about being in charge of the conversation. It's about building a relationship—which is what quality time is truly about. It takes effort and consistency, but it doesn't actually require a massive investment of hours. And the best part? You can structure things you already do every day into quality time.

The Family Table

I know the family dinner has gone by the wayside for many. More and more meals are eaten on the run or with the TV blaring in the background. It's time to pull the family back together.

Try designating just one meal a week to building a relationship. Turn off the TV, remove the headsets, and set phones aside. To make this work, you need two ground rules:

1. **Everyone gets an opportunity to speak, (and all opinions are valid).** You might hear things that make it hard to keep quiet, but stay calm. Use that information for a one-on-one talk later.
2. **No one is allowed to ridicule or make fun of anyone else.** This must be a safe time.

First, '*valid*' doesn't mean you agree with them. It means they are allowed to say it without being shut down immediately. **You are gathering intel.** If you jump down their throat at the dinner table, they'll likely never tell you anything again. Save the '*Hammer*' for later; the table is for the '*Heart*'.

You may find the conversation difficult at first. So have a few light topics ready to jump-start things. And if you can't find a night that works, try a Saturday brunch, a Sunday lunch or have a game night or pizza night. Something fun will make everyone want to participate.

Most importantly, **if someone has to sacrifice an activity to make it happen, make sure that person is you—the adult—and not the child.**

The Captive Audience

Every time you get in the car with your children, you have a captive audience. They have nowhere they can go and nothing to do. This is the perfect time to talk and, more importantly, to listen. If they are lost in their earbuds, ask them to share one of them so you can enjoy the music too. Ask them questions about what you're hearing. Discuss the lyrics. Who is the group or performer? Even if you don't know the artists, your child does—let them be the expert for a change.

And don't be too hard on the kids for what you may hear in the music. If your values are offended, don't blame them. They are under immense peer pressure these days. Don't be afraid to push the topic to a better time. If there are others in the car, like their friends, it might be better to reschedule your talk. Just don't forget about it.

You want to have a better understanding of their side and be able to give them some options. For example, the lyrics to a song may be disrespectful or they could be downright nasty. You wouldn't want to skip over it just because there's a friend in the car. Find another time to talk about it. Again, get your talking points together and be prepared. Define words in the lyrics that may be hurtful or dangerous. Is the material criminal? What are the consequences for these types of actions? In my day, sex was the prevailing topic of concern. Today, they are listening to music that promotes murder of police officers. That's a *huge* issue that you must address.

Remember, the goal is not to embarrass the child or to exercise your authority. And it's not about being the '*Music Police,*' it's to be the '*Reality Check.*' Ask them: 'Do you really believe what this guy is saying, or is he just selling an image?' You want them to analyze the message, not just mindlessly consume it.

Every song you discuss and every meal you share is a brick in the wall of the child's character. You aren't just 'hanging out'; you are investing in your relationships and teaching them how to engage others. If they can talk to you about a difficult lyric, they can eventually talk to a boss about a difficult project.

Chapter 5: The Ledger Lesson

(Why "No" is a Financial Fact, Not a Mean Answer)

As a child, I remember asking my mother how much money she made. She was indignant; she told me it was none of my business. I was hurt, but I got over it, and I never asked again. But the result was that I grew up never knowing much about handling money. Years later when I found myself divorced, I was in a predicament—humiliated actually, because I had to rely on my ex-husband to tell me which bills to pay.

I decided my children would not have that same handicap.

From "I Want" to "We Can't"

Our kids were used to a two-income family where they got pretty much what they wanted. After the divorce, half that income was gone, but the bills remained the same. They didn't understand why I was suddenly saying "no" all the time.

Instead of arguing, I laid out the bills. I showed them…

- The balances and payments due;
- The dates they had to be paid;
- My actual paycheck stubs.

I had them write out the checks and balance the ledger. It didn't take long for them to realize there simply wasn't enough money. This lesson was a huge help in stopping the begging for things we couldn't afford.

The "Want" vs. "Need"

Here's another reality of family life. Kids grow! And when they do, you have to clothe them. The issue with my daughter was that I had saved the money to provide her several nice "generic" outfits but she wanted designer brands. I tried to reason with her but she was really set on having those designer jeans with the fancy pockets and custom stitching. I offered to upgrade the generic ones on my sewing machine but that was rejected. I explained the money I had set aside really wasn't enough to cover a complete wardrobe of designer clothes. I wanted her to have input in the choices we made, especially when it directly affected her. But short of insisting on the generic brands, I couldn't sway her. I decided to let her have her way and suffer the consequences. I gave her the money set aside for her clothes and made it clear there was nothing more.

So, she went shopping. I was going to buy her four pair of jeans and three tops. But her tastes were pretty extravagant. She had money for two pair of designer jeans and one top. She was very excited and pleased with herself when she showed me her haul. However, after a few weeks of "wear it today and wash it tonight," the designer label was no longer important. That was a tough semester! But it did the job, training her to think about more important things than designer labels.

"Need" vs. "Need"

Susan learned the value of money that semester. But I also learned a tough lesson. Her brother had a growth spurt that changed his shoe size by two whole sizes. He was a big boy and he graduated from the boy's section to the men's section at a very inopportune time financially. I too had a shoe need. My work shoes had a crack across the sole which quickly became a gaping hole. Money was tighter than usual I remember and I was just trying to hold off on the spending another month. But when kids outgrow their shoes, they can no longer wear them. He had to have new ones. Mine were uncomfortable and kept my nylons wet most of the time, but I *could* wear them and get by. So, mom wore her old shoes and son got a new pair of tennies.

I didn't tell my kids I was wearing shoes with holes in them. My son *needed* those sneakers and I wasn't about to make him feel guilty about it. Don't get me wrong, I'm not a martyr. I hated every minute of that time, but that's what a leader does. That's what a parent does.

We take the hit so others can move forward.

Sharing the Solution

This transparency didn't just explain the "no"; it explained the sacrifice. It helped them understand why I had to take the second job that I worked for the next six years. Because they saw the problems, they could be part of the solution.

Don't shield your children from the financial reality of the home; use it to train them for the realities of the world. Teaching them early might save them from a lifetime of credit card debt later.

Chapter 6: High-Stakes Parenting

(When the "System" Isn't Enough)

There is a terrifying moment in parenting when the stakes move beyond messy rooms or missed curfews. It's the moment a child realizes they can use the world as a weapon against you—like threatening to run away or threatening to report you to the authorities.

When my children reached this point, I had to be very clear: I would not back down to a child or a "system" that didn't understand my higher goal. My goal was to raise respectable citizens, and I was prepared to pay the price to see it through.

Calling the Bluff

When a child threatens to report you for child abuse because you are exercising discipline, it causes havoc. My response was honest: "You could cause trouble for this family, but if you do, you will be the one removed, and *we will proceed without you*".

The same applied to the threat of running away. I told my child, "I can't sit around worrying about it 24 hours a day. If you decide to run, I can't stop you. I can't be your shadow 24/7. But there is a rule for running away. If that's what you're going to do, you must leave your keys on the table and lock the door behind you. If you leave, you leave, but the rest of the family will be safe". It sounds cold, but it tells the child that while you are concerned, their choices have consequences that affect everyone.

My son did run away—sort of. A few days later he put his keys on the table and locked the door behind him. My daughter and I were asleep and didn't hear a thing until the doorbell woke me up at 2AM. I peeked through the peephole in the door and saw him standing there. I didn't answer the door or call to him or anything. After a couple more rings, he seemed to understand he was out for the night. He sat on the porch until I was dressed and leaving for work that morning. Of course I didn't get any sleep. I was continually quietly checking to make sure he was okay.

That only happened once, thank goodness. It's terrifying to leave your child on the front porch by himself all night long. But we survived it.

The Ultimate Intervention

One of the hardest nights of my life was the night I called the police on my own son. He was becoming incorrigible, and the situation had become unlivable. I had to insist—

loudly—that the officers arrest him because the current laws made them hesitant. They told me he'd have to be picked up from Juvenile within four hours. No problem! As soon as they left with him, I left the house so they couldn't call me to pick him up any earlier (this was before cell phones). I needed him to feel the full weight of the law while he was still young enough to outlive the mistake.

The Hardest Conversation: Suicide

My family is beset with suicides. I have five family members who have committed suicide and I've seen the carnage after the fact. From this experience, I have learned three truths:

1. If a person even mentions suicide as a possibility—even in passing—they can do it.
2. If a person's mind is set on it, you cannot stop them.
3. If a person is threatening suicide, he/she is (probably subconsciously) manipulating your feelings to get their own way. This is a dangerous cycle where the "stakes" must constantly be raised to get the same emotional response from you. If the threat stops working, the person may move to a half-hearted attempt, and eventually, they may feel they have to actually commit suicide just to regain control. I knew I had to stop the stakes at the bottom level.

Those are the reasons I chose the path I took when my 16-year-old son was thinking about it. He had purchased a gun from someone at school and I found it in a drawer one day while he was out. This is a topic I could not mess around with. I couldn't tolerate even the suggestion of a compromise. I had to make my stand firm and clear.

I didn't offer platitudes. I didn't tantrum or cause a huge scene. I simply detailed exactly how it would devastate me, his sister, and his grandparents. I told him the devastation it had caused in our extended family. Then I told him how it would affect us. I would have to go on living—working, going to church, raising his sister. I would be the most miserable mother for the rest of my life, but I would be alive… and he would be dead.

I told him I was getting rid of the gun and he was not to bring another into my house. And I made him promise that if he decided to do it, he would not do it in my home. I could not live in a home where my child killed himself.

Parenting can be a battlefield. It isn't about being liked; it's about ensuring they survive their own poor choices so they have a chance at a future. Perhaps this is not the way you would choose to handle a situation like this, but I felt it was *my* only option. When a threat no longer brings about the desired response, the stakes have to be raised. Over time, the stakes progression runs out and the only option is to commit suicide. I knew I had to stop the stakes at the bottom level.

And don't think for a minute that I didn't lay awake many nights worrying if I had done the right thing. In the end, my son went to a therapist and I didn't hear the word again until he was grown and married with his own children. He said I handled it perfectly. I doubt that is true, but I did handle it the only way I could.

Chapter 7: The United Front and the Long Game

(Divorce, Adulthood, and the Finish Line)

The Tag-Team Effect

For those who are not doing it alone, you have a responsibility to each other. The best gift you can give your children is to love each other and stand united.

I have seen too many families where "Dad is the disciplinarian" and "Mom is the caregiver". This is unfair to everyone. Dads become unyielding because they only deal with the negatives, and Moms burn out because there is no end to the caregiving. You must be a **tag-team**.

Both parents have to be everything to their children—the hammer and the heart.

But what happens when that union breaks?

Divorce Decorum

When a marriage ends, the parenting shouldn't. If you are divorced, the stakes for the "United Front" are actually higher, not lower. You must maintain a boundary of respect for the sake of the child's identity.

Never, under any circumstances, criticize your ex-spouse in front of your children. It doesn't make you look better; it only makes the child feel like half of who they are is "bad." You are teaching them how to handle conflict and disappointment—show them how to do it with dignity. A "Respectable Citizen" isn't built on the ruins of their other parent. If you can't be a united front in the same house, be a united front in your standards of character.

The Myth of 18: Moving from Commander to Consultant

We have this idea in our culture that 18 is a magic number where parenting ends—that you simply "finish" the job and walk away. It isn't. You don't stop being a parent when they get a diploma or a driver's license. Your influence continues, but your title changes.

This is the hand-off: You shift from "Commander" to "Consultant."

As a commander, you gave orders. As a consultant, you give "quotes." When your adult children come to you with a problem, you don't solve it for them; you point them back to the tools you gave them. You ask, "What does your ledger look like?" or "What do you see when you look in the mirror?" One of my biggest lessons was realizing even as they become adults, they are still watching. They are watching how you handle your own life, your own money, and your own mistakes. This is why the lessons of this book are so important—they aren't just for toddlers; they are for life.

The Finish Line: Respectable Citizens

At the end of the day, we aren't raising "good kids." We are raising future adults. If you spend eighteen years trying to be their best friend, you will likely end up with an adult who doesn't know how to be a friend to anyone.

The goal of all this "negativeness," the energy-draining work, the discipline, and the hard talks is to produce an adult who can stand on their own two feet. An adult who respects others, understands the value of a dollar, and takes responsibility for their actions.

If you've done your job, you won't just have a child you love; you'll have an adult you actually **like**. And when that day comes, you can finally put down that encyclopedia of "my kids won't," look at the adult standing in front of you, and know that every ounce of allotted energy you spent was worth it.

A Final Note from the author:

The Limits of Control

I have shared these stories and these suggested rules because they worked for me, and I believe they are a valid way to build a foundation of respect and responsibility. But I have to be honest with you: even when you do everything "right," you don't always win the battle.

Seven years ago, I lost my daughter to a drug overdose.

It is the most painful reality a parent can endure. For a long time, I questioned every decision I ever made. But here is the hard truth I had to face: We are not the commanders of our children's bodies; we are the stewards of their training. We give them the map, we give them the tools, and we give them the boundaries—but ultimately, they are the ones who walk the path.

I didn't write this book to promise you a "perfect" child. I wrote it to help you become a parent who looks in the mirror and knows, with absolute certainty, you did your job. You gave them the truth. You gave them discipline. You gave them real love. The rest is up to them.

Appendix 1:

The Practical Toolkit

- **The Discipline Inventory:** Have your child list four things they love (positive reinforcement) and four things they hate (negative consequences). Use this list to take the guesswork out of rewards and punishments.
- **The Energy Audit:** Real parenting requires demonstrating commitment by reviewing homework, checking chores, and listening more than talking—even when you are dog-tired.
- **The Ledger Lesson:** Don't shield children from financial reality; show them the bills and the paycheck stubs to teach the difference between "Wants" and "Needs."

Appendix 2:

The Parenting Cheat Sheet

(Managing Behavior, Preparing Adults)

The Three Pillars of Training

- **Training:** Giving children the tools to make a good choice before they are faced with a bad one.
- **Instruction:** Setting the standard for how to move through the world and teaching acceptable manners and social behaviors.
- **Education:** Teaching children the hard lessons at the lower end of the spectrum to save them from major troubles they cannot outlive later.

The Golden Rules of Discipline

- **The Two-Strike Rule:** If you have to say something more than twice, the child is in control. The third time you speak, you move to "consequences" rather than "negotiation."
- **The Double Trouble Rule:** If a child gets in trouble with an outside authority (e.g., teacher or babysitter), the consequence is doubled at home.
- **The Mirror Method:** For behaviors that are unacceptable, perhaps a mirror will allow the child to experience the reality of their own behavior firsthand.